BUSINESS ETHICS

BUSINESS ETHICS

A Guide for Managers

Elizabeth P Tierney

KOGAN PAGE

YOURS TO HAVE AND TO HOLD
BUT NOT TO COPY

The publication you are reading is protected by copyright law. This means that the publisher could take you and your employer to court and claim heavy legal damages if you make unauthorised photocopies from these pages. Photocopying copyright material without permission is no different from stealing a magazine from a newsagent, only it doesn't seem like theft.

The Copyright Licensing Agency (CLA) is an organisation which issues licences to bring photocopying within the law. It has designed licensing services to cover all kinds of special needs in business, education and government.

If you take photocopies from books, magazines and periodicals at work your employer should be licensed with CLA. Make sure you are protected by a photocopying licence.

The Copyright Licensing Agency Limited, 90 Tottenham Court Road, London, W1P OLP. Tel: 0171 436 5931. Fax: 0171 436 3986.

First published in 1996

Apart from any fair dealing for the purposes of research or private study, or criticism or review, as permitted under the Copyright, Designs and Patents Act, 1988, this publication may only be reproduced, stored or transmitted, in any form or by any means, with the prior permission in writing of the publishers, or in the case of reprographic reproduction in accordance with the terms and licences issued by the CLA. Enquiries concerning reproduction outside those terms should be sent to the publishers at the undermentioned address:

Kogan Page Limited
120 Pentonville Road
London N1 9JN

© Elizabeth P Tierney, 1996

British Library Cataloguing in Publication Data
A CIP record for this book is available from the British Library.

ISBN 0 7494 1892 3

Typeset by BookEns Ltd, Royston, Herts
Printed and bound in Great Britain by
Biddles Ltd, Guildford and King's Lynn

Contents

Introduction 7

1. **Why Create an Ethical Working Environment?** 9
   You were given standards on your first job 9
   You were given standards during your childhood 11
   You were given standards in your current job 12
   You provide standards for others 13
   Company materials describe standards 16
   Have you addressed ethics in the workplace? 17
   How do you establish ethical standards? 18
   What are ethical dilemmas? 19
   The case of the boss's daughter 20
   Ethical dilemmas are a fact of business life 22
   Resolving ethical dilemmas causes discomfort 24
   What are the consequences of the discomfort? 26
   Ignore ethics at your peril 26
   Is ethics a threat or an opportunity? 28

2. **Why Do People Make Unethical Decisions?** 31
   We are taught to be good 31
   We aren't always good 32
   We have diverse standards 36
   We are human 37
   What are the implications of those differences in the workplace? 38
   Motivation theories help us to understand ourselves 40

Applying theories helps us to understand ourselves 44
Pressures may cause us to act unethically 44
We forget to think about values 45
Insight is often based on hindsight 46

3. **What Does Unethical Behaviour Cost?** 49
Some say that there are no costs to unethical behaviour 49
But are there no costs whatsoever? 50
Maybe we would deceive, if we were better at it 51
There are costs to being deceitful 52
The costs of being unethical in business are significant 52
What are some internal consequences once trust is lost? 55
Trust matters 62
But what about the cost of unethical behaviour to an organisation itself? 63
What have companies done to redeem their good names? 64

4. **How Can You Create an Ethical Working Environment?** 67
Step 1. Make the decision to commit to ethics 68
Step 2 Recognise that you are a role model by definition, by your actions and by your values 68
Step 3. Assume the responsibility for instilling ethical behaviour 76
Step 4. Determine what you consider to be ethical practice 76
Step 5. Articulate your values 78
Step 6. Train your staff 80
Step 7. Encourage open communication 81
Step 8. Be consistent 82

Further Reading from Kogan Page 85

Introduction

Before you begin this book about business ethics, know that there are some managers who consider the notion of relating ethics and business as a joke. Others view the juxtaposition of the words as impossible or improbable. Still others consider discussions of ethics as irrelevant. And still others avoid talking about ethics because of some vague fear that they will be overheard, the anxiety stemming from the likelihood that such conversations might be construed as an admission of guilt or wrongdoing. Nothing could be further from the truth.

More and more forward-thinking business people from around the world and from diverse public and private industry sectors are recognising that the 2000-year-old debate about ethics and commerce should be addressed anew.

Unlike their doubting colleagues, these businessmen and businesswomen view the recent refocusing on values, on how we do business, as an opportunity for organisations to re-examine what they stand for and where they are going in order to compete successfully in a complex and competitive global economy.

Such managers do not see discussions of ethics and business as a joke, as a threat or as a weakness, but rather as a natural outgrowth of the current movements in industry towards excellence and quality.

This book is not a philosophical treatise. It is a guide to assist managers in understanding business ethics by raising and answering four questions:

Business Ethics

1. Why create an ethical working environment?
2. Why do people make unethical decisions?
3. What are some of the costs associated with unethical behaviour?
4. How can you create an ethical working environment?

The purpose of this book is to underline the importance of ethical decision-making for you personally and for your company and to clarify what a significant role you as a manager play in creating an ethical working environment.

To develop such an environment, you are asked to find time to reflect on a number of your own experiences and to answer some questions. Throughout the book, the following words are used interchangeably: values, ethics and standards. Values refer to principles, standards to the degree of excellence and ethics to rules of conduct.

The book is designed to be interactive. There are questions to answer and scenarios to analyse which are included to assist you in creating an ethical working environment.

CHAPTER 1
Why Create an Ethical Working Environment?

Let's begin our discussion of the role of ethics in business by thinking about some of the standards that you live and work by and how you acquired those standards. This requires some deep reflection on your part, but the results, you will agree, are worth the effort.

You were given standards on your first job

One way to begin your reflection process might be to remember the first few jobs that you ever had.

> Perhaps you were a newspaper deliverer or a child minder. Perhaps you were a sales assistant in a local newsagent, or a barman or barmaid.
> Perhaps you entered the labour market at a different level, as a management trainee, for instance, or even as a consultant.

Think back to whatever those early jobs were, and name two or three of them:

_____

_____

Business Ethics

Now try to recollect the first hour or first day or first week of each of those jobs, when the boss in each case explained the rules of employment. You may recall that, in fact, the offer of employment was contingent upon your accepting those rules:

'If you want to deliver papers, you'll have to be ready to work at 5.00am. Agreed?' Once you said yes, perhaps you were admonished to 'put them through the letter box, not in the bushes.'

If you were a sales assistant, perhaps you were encouraged to 'smile at every customer.'

If you were a child minder, the rules were probably something like, 'He'll try to stay up until nine, but get him to bed at half past eight.'

If you were a management trainee, in an office setting, you may have been expected to 'write a weekly progress report.'

If you were a consultant, you may have been directed to 'submit your recommendations in two weeks.'

So, looking back at the first days of those early jobs that you have listed above, write a few of the initial instructions that you can recall being given by your boss. In other words, spell out the requirements of the positions:

_____

_____
_____

_____

What you have written above were, in effect, the rules, guidelines, and/or expectations, which represented your boss's standards for doing business:

'Put a smile in your voice when you talk to a customer.'

Why Create an Ethical Working Environment?

'Use the company letterhead for external communications only, not for internal memos.'

'Plan to work late on Thursdays.'

Whatever the scope or nature of the admonitions or expectations, presumably you were expected to work according to them.

You were given standards during your childhood

Besides the directions that were given to you in your first jobs, write a few other rules or parameters that governed some of your actions, especially those outside the workplace:

_____

_____

_____

_____

Who were the people who gave you those rules?

_____

_____

_____

As you have probably indicated, those other standards derived from a variety of sources, from different aspects of your life. We have been raised according to a litany of rules and recommendations from family, teachers, coaches, religious leaders, and from government. If your list of standards is to be more inclusive, it might reflect such admonitions as:

'Don't leave dirty dishes in the sink.'

'Look both ways before crossing the street.'

Business Ethics

'Say thank you when someone does something nice for you.'

'Tell the truth.'

'Try not to hurt anyone.'

By now you are probably wondering what all this talk about crossing streets and leaving dirty dishes has to do with ethics in the workplace. Ethics is about standards, and the point of having you ask and answer questions or make lists is to encourage you to reflect on the guidelines that you have been exposed to in your lifetime as well as on their diverse origins.

You were given standards in your current job

Having reflected briefly on the earlier days of your work experience and childhood, focus now on some more recent instructions that you have been given by your employers. Concentrate on those instructions that were spelled out for you in the first few days, hours or weeks of your current position, as well as on those that constituted your induction into the organisation and to the job you now hold.

What were some of the guidelines that were given to you in the early days of your current position?

_____

_____

_____

_____

Tick the method(s) by which those guidelines were made clear to you:

- ☐ new employee briefing
- ☐ formal induction programme
- ☐ job description
- ☐ informal chat

☐ staff handbook
☐ trial and error
☐ another approach.

You provide standards for others

In the preceding pages, you have reflected on how you received the guidelines by which you live and work. Now, take another perspective. In your role as manager, think about the people who report to you at the present time. Consider some of the guidelines that you think are important for them to know, the standards that you set out for them in their first days of employment with you.

List some of the guidelines that you establish for your staff:

_____
_____
_____
_____

What method(s) do you use to disseminate this information?

_____
_____
_____
_____

How do the methods for dissemination that you use differ from those you have experienced?

_____
_____
_____
_____

Business Ethics

In your own career, you have probably been through the typical induction process. This usually includes discussion of benefits: pension rights, health insurance, sick leave, holiday entitlement, expense reimbursement procedures and appraisal systems.

Do you believe that these topics should be a priority in an effective and meaningful induction process?

                Yes ☐   No ☐

If yes, why?

_____

_____

_____

If no, why?

_____

_____

_____

What additional topics might you include in the list of induction items?

_____

_____

_____

Now ask yourself why you, as a manager, take the time to provide this information to a new employee:

_____

_____

_____

Why Create an Ethical Working Environment?

In your response to that last query, it is likely that you have listed some of the very same reasons that parents or first bosses give when they are asked why they set standards or establish rules. Don't feel that this is at all extraordinary. Like teachers, doctors, parents or other bosses before you, you are probably:

- seeking to clarify to the new employee how you expect something to be done;
- trying to save time by not answering the same questions over and over again;
- putting new staff at their ease so that they will know the 'rules of the game';
- trying to simplify procedures;
- avoiding misunderstandings;
- anticipating problems;
- protecting and supporting staff rather than having them feel frustrated, hurt or angry.

For example, to avoid confusion about holiday entitlements, you could decide to clarify accrual systems in advance. You might explain procedures: how to phone in when ill; how to use the new fax or photocopy system; what to do in an emergency. You might also explain company policy about discrimination, bidding or internal promotions. In essence, your rationale for explaining is to ease the new employee into a system, either yours or the company's, and into the firm's culture. Corporate culture as a concept refers in part to the notion that organisations, like societies, have their own values and norms, to which the members adhere.

You are well aware of the idea of corporate culture if you have had experience working in more than one organisation. You know how important the induction process is for you and for the employee. You are well aware that every organisation has its own system, its own way of doing business, its own particular environment. Compare organisations for which you have worked. Think about how each one of them had its own way of doing things, even simple things like how to answer the phone, whether or not to use first names or titles, or how to disseminate information. Firms are different in the way that they operate.

Company materials describe standards

Job descriptions, staff handbooks, policy manuals, and appraisal forms are all mechanisms for providing guidelines and for setting company standards. They spell out the expectations for how business is to be conducted in an organisation. In one way or another, the intent of these documents is to clarify the organisational structure and to indicate parameters for employee behaviour. These may include providing such information as: Who is in charge? Of what? What's that person's telephone extension? This type of data is particularly important in a large organisation which has many people in many highly specialised roles. An employee might need to know, for example, who is in charge of personnel. Is there an assistant? What's the office number? What does a particular request form look like?

Exclusions from, as well as the contents of, a company's statement of guidelines can reflect management values. Guidelines make clear what management deems to be important or unimportant, what is or is not a priority. For example, if you delivered the newspaper, how it was folded may have been less important than its being put through the letterbox. While timeliness may be emphasised by an organisation, precision may not be referred to at all.

If your company has an employee handbook, examine it, and then list what it considers to be major company priorities. These priorities may be stated or implied.*

---

* See *How to Write a Staff Manual* in this series.

Why Create an Ethical Working Environment?

Having examined the handbook again, state what the company does *not* appear to regard as a major priority:

_____

_____

_____

_____

Have you addressed ethics in the workplace?

Now, you ask, what does all this talk about induction have to do with a company's ethics? A great deal. You have reflected on the induction process that you experienced and on the one that you now provide for your own staff. In so doing, you have assessed the content of the written material that you distribute, such as handbooks or guidelines. Assess any visual material that you might distribute as well.

Having thought about all that, consider the following:

- Do you refer to ethics in the induction process?
- Do you refer to values in the induction process?
- Do you refer to standards in the induction process?
- Is there a section in the handbook entitled, 'Handling an Ethical Problem' or some such similar heading?
- Has your company codes of conduct or codes of practice?
- Are there any procedures designed to assist staff when they are confronted by unethical practices?
- Are there people to contact for advice, if an employee is faced with a dilemma?

If your company's induction process makes reference to ethics, values or standards in its handbook or with a code, then take heart. Yours is one of an increasing number of organisations which already acknowledge the importance of addressing the ethical or the values dimension of work.

Frequently, however, the only acknowledgement that ethics is an issue for a company is the addition of a single sentence or word to an existing mission statement or credo. Instead of the appending of a few well-turned phrases, what should be occurring in organisations is the development of detailed policies, or a serious commitment to training about ethical dilemmas and the establishment of company-wide procedures for handling such issues.

How do you establish ethical standards?

- With yourself

Suppose concern for ethical standards in the workplace is a new idea for you. True, we have been discussing handbooks, but an important point to bear in mind is that increasing awareness about the importance of ethics in the office is not about adding sections or language to handbooks. That increasing awareness about creating an ethical environment begins with you, the manager, thinking; with you, the manager, reflecting on your values and about how and what kinds of values you want to instil in your organisation.

Tackling values issues requires that before a word about ethics is put on paper or uttered at a meeting, you should reflect on some basics about management, about yourself, about people and about relationships. When you do so reflect, you will soon recognise how frequently ethical dilemmas occur in business.

- With time

To consider ethics as an essential fact of life in business, you, as a busy manager, need to devote more time to thinking about it. Finding that time isn't easy. We all get caught up in the demands of the day, the phone calls to return, the meetings to attend, the people to meet. It is not surprising that most managers view their days as filled with endless decision-taking. As a result, they may forget the importance of building in time for reflection, not just in the car or bus on the way to work but at the office as well.

Why Create an Ethical Working Environment?

- With reflection

Therefore, let's stop to underline that important and often forgotten aspect of management: reflection. Devoting time to thinking rather than to doing is an essential element of the manager's role. In the process of asking questions about the state of ethics in the company, it is vital.

To reinforce the point that managers tend to view 'doing' rather than 'reflecting' as a priority, think about some of the words that you see in other people's CVs and that you may use in your own CV as well.

What words do you use to describe what you do?

_____

_____

- Did you write: design, implement, organise, meet?
- Did you write: reflect, weigh, consider, ponder, evaluate?

Most likely you chose words like those in the first group. That's understandable. We see ourselves as action people, as doers. It is also an indication of why many managers, and, therefore, many companies have yet to tackle the elusive issues of ethics. Many managers haven't made or found the time to reflect on, or think about, ethics and values. Consequently, they haven't determined how to provide guidelines and support to the people who report to them, when they find themselves in the murk, mire or quicksand of ethical dilemmas.

What are ethical dilemmas?

Here are some examples of what might be ethical dilemmas:

- Whether or not you should accept an expensive weekend from one of your company's suppliers.
- Whether or not you should give clients the results of research that you know they want to hear rather than what you know to be true.

19

Business Ethics

- Whether or not you should sell a product that gives you a higher commission rather than serve the needs of a particular customer.
- Whether or not you should manipulate figures to achieve a desired end-of-year result or target.
- Whether or not to ask employees to withhold certain information.

What other ethical dilemmas can you think of?

_____

_____

_____

_____

_____

_____

You know that ethical dilemmas are tough problems to solve. They are worrisome. They are common. They are frequently full of intangibles. They may involve harming someone, and they can have a variety of implications for different stakeholders.

To reiterate, ethical dilemmas are situations that are not black and white; they are grey. Resolving dilemmas requires us to make decisions when we are not guided by laws, regulations, statutes, or absolute truths. Ethical dilemmas are fraught with 'what ifs', with 'maybes', with 'on the one hand, we should ..., but on the other hand if we do ..., but then again, if I don't, they might ...'

The case of the boss's daughter

Let me cite a personal experience with an ethical dilemma. I was a senior manager in a large public service organisation. One day the boss, who was also the board president, phoned me to determine whether or not I had received his daughter's application for a current opening. I indicated that it had,

Why Create an Ethical Working Environment?

indeed, come in, but that the closing date for the paperwork had passed.

'Oh,' he said, 'you're not going to let a qualified candidate be excluded because of a closing date, are you?' Then he added quickly, 'but let me not interfere.'

As I hung up the phone, I replayed the conversation in my mind and pondered the implications.

Later that day, the union president, who thrived on turmoil, asked to see me. Despite my offering him a chair, he chose to stand by the door that he had just closed and said, 'I hear that the boss's daughter has applied for the opening. You're not going to consider her, are you? She worked here years ago, and there were problems. The place will be up in arms if you take her back.' He smilingly added, 'I just wanted to let you know and to help.' Then he turned on his heel and left.

If you were faced with this situation, what would you have done?

_____

_____

_____

_____

All I know is that I wanted to talk to someone, but who could I go to? I said to myself, 'Think through what you have heard from both parties to determine what is the truth, to determine what is the fair thing to do.'

I attempted to tease out all the alternatives and to figure out who would be affected by whatever I did.

Even without knowing the details of the organisation, which groups or individuals do you think might have been affected by my decision?

_____

_____

Other than the issue of the closing date, there was nothing in this problem that was covered by company policy, statute or law. There was no prohibition against hiring family members. I was on my own, without a handbook, with no guidelines, no policy and no procedures. Just my conscience.

Ethical dilemmas are a fact of business life

The case that I described is not unusual. Most of us are faced with dilemmas at some time, perhaps often. Along with the other examples of situations listed earlier, consider what you would do if any of the following happened to you:

- You discover that one of your company's products is defective, and that the line manager responsible for its production is aware of the situation, but has said nothing;
- You notice a flaw in a new product design, but when you report it, you are ignored by the person responsible;
- You become aware of the misuse of company property by one of your superiors;
- You find yourself under continuing pressure from a superior to mislead a client;
- You are invited to an elegant golf club by a vendor who is a brother-in-law of your MD. You know that he is shipping your company defective merchandise;
- You know that several members of the sales department are manipulating figures to meet their sales quotas.

Again, what would you do? On a continuum would you ignore it? Would you try to change it? If you couldn't, would you leave the company over it? Tough questions. The reality is that such ethical dilemmas may occur anywhere or any time: in the marketing department, the human resource department, the accountancy department, anywhere, any time.

Why Create an Ethical Working Environment?

Describe a situation in your department or company which required you to have come to terms with an ethical dilemma:

_____
_____
_____
_____

What was at issue?

_____
_____
_____
_____

Who could have been affected by the decision? In other words, who were all the stakeholders?

_____
_____
_____
_____

As the person who had to resolve the dilemma, what options did you have?

_____
_____
_____
_____
_____

Business Ethics

Who, if anyone, helped you to take the decision?

_____
_____
_____

Did you finally resolve the dilemma?

_____
_____
_____

How did you resolve it?

_____
_____
_____
_____

How did you feel during the decision-making process?

_____
_____
_____
_____

Resolving ethical dilemmas causes discomfort

You may be reluctant to answer that last question because it is about feelings. Emotions may seem to be a trivial issue in the tough world of business. But they are a serious matter. For most of us, when we are faced with a dilemma, selecting the wisest option is not easy, and it is natural to feel unsure, especially when emotions are involved. We may feel angry,

Why Create an Ethical Working Environment?

frustrated, bewildered, resentful or annoyed to have to deal with the situation in the first place, because we have no ready solution to hand.

When I grappled with the situation that was developing around the application of the boss's daughter, I weighed the options. I tried desperately to sort out what was fair and right. Of course, I was part of the equation, too. What price was I going to pay for the final decision? Should I honour the closing date? After all, was it carved in stone? Was she the best candidate? Was she a better candidate than the others? What was her history with the organisation? Were there records? Were they comprehensive, unbiased? Was I being pressured? By whom? Would I appear to be a pawn of the union? Of the boss? What new problems would be brought about by my decision? What precedents would I be setting? My brain spun as the questions developed exponentially.

I had a headache. I was preoccupied. I expended time and energy trying to decide what to do. What compounded the problem was that I didn't know whom I could trust to talk through the pros and cons, or who could see more far-reaching consequences than I could. One minute I was sure of what to do. The next minute I thought of another alternative. Was I weighing what was best for the organisation? Was I weighing what was best for me? Was I weighing what was best for the candidate? Was what was best for the candidate also what was best for the organisation?

The problem came home with me. I slept badly. I was irritable. Back at the office, other tasks were put on the back burner. My patience with other organisational issues was nil. In essence, I was angry and felt threatened, and yet I knew I had a responsibility to the organisation.

So, if you skipped that question about how you felt during the process of resolving the dilemma facing you, please go back to it now and recall your emotions during the process. If you felt exhilarated by the challenge, bravo, but more than likely, you felt drained. I know that I was, as I wrestled with the alternatives and implications over that 36-hour period.

Business Ethics

What are the consequences of the discomfort?

Let's think in terms of your staff. Assuming that your employees recognise that they are on the horns of a dilemma when they are beset by an ethical problem, and are fatigued by the struggle required to resolve it, then assess the consequences of that battle on morale, performance or productivity. Using my situation, remember how I described my feelings as I struggled with the decision about the boss's daughter. Think about your own experience in resolving a dilemma. If you experienced discomfort, too, then multiply that discomfort by the number of people who report to you. Now, multiply that figure by the number of dilemmas that each person might face on a daily, weekly or monthly basis. This will give you an idea of the potential for unhappiness and loss of focus.

Although there is no mathematical formula to guide us, if resolving ethical dilemmas is time-consuming and emotionally draining, what is the impact on your ability to achieve your departmental or organisational goals or targets? On the one hand, you may say, there is no time for so much soul searching. Make the decision. Get on with it and live with the consequences. You have a job to do. 'Time is money.' On the other hand, you might be concerned about the impact of that discomfort on morale or on motivation.

Ignore ethics at your peril

We live in a competitive environment, a global village. As managers, we have to reflect on and recognise that ethical dilemmas are a reality. So, too, is coming to terms with the necessity of establishing ethical standards a fact of business life. Although we may prefer to ignore the fact that ethical dilemmas are the norm rather than the exception, and that they are difficult to resolve, we overlook the ethical implications of our decisions at our peril. Not only is this so for your staff's emotional well-being, but because in the bluntest of terms, you might become headline news.

Why Create an Ethical Working Environment?

From the beginning of this book, you have been asked to be introspective and to reflect on yourself, on who you are and on what you do. For the moment, let's look outwards rather than inwards. Let's take a look at the bigger picture, the external reality in which you and your organisation operate.

Are the names of the following individuals, products or organisations familiar to you?

    Union Carbide at Bhopal, India
    BCCI
    Exxon Valdez
    Michael Miliken
    Robert Maxwell
    Barlow Clowes
    Barings Bank
    Nestlé's Infant Formula

If they are, what do they have in common?

_____

_____

_____

Add a few more names:

_____

_____

_____

The names that you have added to the list have presumably also been in the news, as the others have, because of some discovery, dramatic or otherwise, of alleged questionable business practices or decisions.

No one, surely, would like to see his or her own name or company's name on such a list.

While it is easy to be melodramatic about ethics or to overstate the case, in terms of the external reality, ethics is an issue for you, as a manager. The world is smaller; communications and information technology are such that the availability of, speed of and appetite for news means that malfeasance in Oxford can be headlines in Ottawa. Poor ethical decision-making in Tokyo can be seen on cable in London.

Today's journalists are tenacious and mobile, and consumers are demanding. Simultaneously, groups and associations are committed to expressing their concerns and having attention paid to such diverse aspects of life as the quality of our drinking water, our beaches, our air, the well-being of our own and of other species. In addition, there are social movements and lobbyists currently raising awareness about nutrition, disease, ageing, sexuality, disabilities, health and safety. The list is lengthy.

Therefore, from a pragmatic point of view, if one of your corporate decisions is found to be unethical, is determined to have caused harm to individuals, animals, or the environment, you might some day find that you have become, if not bold headlines, then simply news.

We are all subject to the potential of public scrutiny. We take the chance that our own good names are put at risk or our company's reputation is damaged by a potential loss of profitability as we lose customers. As a consequence of such notoriety, we may find that we need to reallocate resources for damage control or repair.

For example, if company X produces a product using poorly paid labour, it won't be long in today's technologically advanced world before such information is widely known. If company Y is doing business in a country with a history of human rights violations, that information will surface as well. Disapproving consumers may take decisions about future purchases and avoid companies X and Y and choose to do business with Z instead.

Is ethics a threat or an opportunity?

People breach confidentiality, obtain and use insider information to their own advantage, do business with corrupt governments, and it may appear that nobody knows or cares. While 'getting caught' or not 'getting caught' is a real concern for a manager, avoidance of scandal is not what should motivate that manager to take ethics seriously.

Values, quality and excellence are all considered international business issues. Ethics is an integral part of each of them. Therefore, what is important is that we view the development of ethical standards as a benefit to the way we do business, not as a hindrance or a threat to success.

When I was confronted by the pressure from my boss and by an implied threat from the union president, I felt alone and confused. I remember thinking 'Who needs this? I've tried to do an honest job, and it comes down to this. I've been reasonable with the union, and it doesn't matter. I've tried to maintain standards, but now the boss is undermining them.'

You could have graphed my motivational level – it was a rapidly descending curve. As a result, for a period of time, I became a disaffected employee.

As managers, what none of us want or need is what I had become: demotivated. I also wondered about my prospects with the organisation. There are no long-term studies of the bottom line implications of addressing ethics. There are no guarantees that an ethical environment leads to higher profits. But there is much to be said for creating an environment in which values are considered to be important. Ethical dilemmas are a fact of business life. They are complex, difficult and uncomfortable to deal with, but we ignore them at our peril.

We may gain a great deal, however, if we address ethical concerns. As you have seen, we have been living with and guided by standards all our lives. Integrity, trust and responsibility are as important to the success of an enterprise as they are to us as individuals. As managers, we have a role to play in instilling those concepts and ensuring that business is done ethically.

If we trust each other, we'll be able to collaborate, to be open. Mistrust leads to fear and limited risk-taking. If we are honest with each other, we will share information even if it is negative, rather than wasting energy second guessing how others might react to our news. If we feel responsibility to each other, to the company, to the community, we will earn respect and as a consequence avoid difficulties or confrontations with stakeholders.

If there is so much to be gained by developing an ethical environment, let's examine why people make unethical decisions.

CHAPTER 2
Why Do People Make Unethical Decisions?

By reflecting on your childhood and on your first jobs, you are quickly reminded of how many significant people in your life encouraged you to be good, gave you standards and provided you with rules. True, you may know of some individuals or have read of some historical figures who had no sense of good or bad. Sociopaths exist in the world. Villains proliferate. Conscienceless characters like Hannibal Lecter do stalk the world, but thankfully they are the exception not the rule.

We are taught to be good

Your family, teachers, headmasters, bosses, scout and guide leaders, religious leaders, political leaders, even your favourite heroes in films, books and TV may have served as examples for you to live by. Regardless of whether you chose Pooh or Superman, or Agatha Christie or Lewis Carroll's Red Queen, each individual modelled good behaviour or, on the other hand, demonstrated what might happen if you violated rules. In other words, along with learning what was right and what was wrong, you also learned that there was a price to be paid if you weren't good, or if you weren't well-behaved, or if you didn't do the right thing.

Who were some of your heroes or heroines?

_____

_____

_____

What qualities of theirs did you want to emulate?

_____

_____

_____

Given all that exposure throughout our childhood to the notion of what it is to be good, you would think that for the rest of our lives we would all have little difficulty making the choice between doing what is right or doing what is wrong. Presumably we know that

 we shouldn't lie,
 we shouldn't steal,
 we shouldn't hurt anyone.

We are also well aware that we should give credit where credit is due. Some of us may have been taught: Do to others as you would have them do to you. Notice the use of the phrase: 'some of us'. Although we all may have standards, they are different for different people. So even though we are taught to be good, we aren't always so.

We aren't always good

While books, films, TV and real people provide us with role models for goodness, those same sources offer us images of evil. Since our focus here is business, let us concentrate on stories that you have read, heard or seen about business people who have not been 'good', who have ignored standards and who have made shameful decisions. Some of their questionable practices involved violating the law, others involved breaches of ethics.

Why Do People Make Unethical Decisions?

As a manager you probably will be faced with tough ethical decisions yourself and will have people reporting to you who have fallen victim to other people's poor decision-making. Some will have made unwise choices themselves. Before we proceed further, it is important to consider why people make bad choices.

Lay-offs, mergers, acquisitions or doing business in foreign countries are complex issues. But not all business decisions are as complicated. To get a sense of some less weighty problems that face you more frequently, let's consider some micro issues. As you read these scenarios, bear in mind that the objectives of studying them are twofold:

1. to note the range of standards and principles that employees and managers have to deal with; and
2. to discover what prompts people to behave in ways that they inherently know to be wrong.

Suppose Manager A learns that an assistant of his, Mary, is using the office phone at least once a week to talk to her sister in California for an hour or so. The manager confronts her with the discovery by asking Mary, if, in fact, she is making these long-distance personal telephone calls.

Mary answers,

> 'Yes. Why? Have I done anything wrong? What's so terrible about my using the phone anyway? The company is big enough to afford it; what's one phone call or two to the States?' Feeling expansive, she adds, 'I phoned my Mum a couple of times last week 'cause I wanted to find out about her trip to Edinburgh. Anyway, it is too early to phone the States before I come to work. What's the problem?'

How do you think her manager should respond?

- [ ] Ignore the situation altogether.
- [ ] Excuse her.
- [ ] Tell her that she can use the phone only in an emergency.

Business Ethics

☐ Tell her that what she is doing is theft.
☐ Do something else:

_____

_____

_____

What are your views on using the company phone to make personal calls?

_____

_____

_____

You can imagine that if we created a continuum of acceptable standards of phone usage, one manager might think that it is acceptable to use the phone any time. Another might consider it acceptable to phone only in an emergency. Yet another might view Mary's behaviour as outright theft, a misuse of company property.

For our purposes, let's have Mary's manager take a hard line and direct her not to make any more personal phone calls, because it is a form of stealing. Outraged, she reacts to his comments by saying,

> 'What? How could that be? I was just using the phone! I don't steal! I never steal! I was brought up not to steal! If you consider my using the phone to talk to my family as stealing, then I suppose I shouldn't take supplies home either. You know, little things like refill pads, envelopes, staplers and pens. I use them to write letters, organise my accounts, write grocery lists, remind myself of chores, or to keep by the phone, to jot down messages. You are just picking on me!
>
> What about the time that John borrowed the computer for the weekend? Was that theft? He needed it to work on his thesis. The PC is company property, too. No one here

was going to need it over a weekend. What's the harm? And anyway, the thesis is for his MBA. The more degrees he gets, the more it'll help the company, right? But then again, he did say to me, off the record, that when he got the degree he was going to look for another position elsewhere.'

Mary's tirade refers to other questionable actions. Some managers would probably view this Pandora's box of issues as silly and inconsequential and would consider that these kinds of petty incident should not be high on anyone's priority lists because there are too many other issues to deal with. Such managers might not be concerned about the cost implications of company property being put to personal use.

Other managers would be aware of the problem, but would prefer to shrug it off by acknowledging that some people take advantage and others don't. Such managers probably view the use of company property as part of the cost of doing business and build it into the price or fee structure. They pass it on to the customer, thus establishing the use of company property for personal use as an inexpensive perk or benefit.

Still other managers might be appalled by an employee's using company property for such purposes; in fact, they believe that it's wrong and are taken aback by such activity. They question the underlying reasons. In other words, on a continuum, some managers may view Mary's actions as wrong, while others may view them as perfectly acceptable or harmless.

If you were in the group who viewed such behaviour as wrong, then you might ask why Mary would do what she did.

Let's consider another scenario. Manager Z asks Norman to submit a report which is to include background, analysis of some data, and recommendations based on the interpretation of that data. Manager Z asks Norman to get the report together within two weeks. Off Norman goes. He delegates the research, analysis and report writing to one of his subordinates, Lisa, who completes the work in ten days and gives the report to Norman. Norman takes Lisa's work, reads it, is satisfied with the content, retypes the cover page to show his name, not Lisa's, and then submits it to Manager Z as if it were his own work. He accepts praise and gives no credit to Lisa, who, in fact, did the research and wrote the report.

Has that ever happened to you?   Yes ☐   No ☐

If it did, what were the circumstances?

_____
_____
_____

What is your reaction to not being given acknowledgement for work that you have done and then seeing someone else being praised for it?

_____
_____
_____

It is possible that you answered that question by saying that subordinates are supposed to do the donkey work, the grunt work. But isn't representing someone else's work as your own a form of theft in the same way as using company property is?

We have diverse standards

There are numerous incidents in the workplace in which otherwise fair, kind, civilised people may be perceived as cheating, lying and stealing as a matter of course. They themselves may not believe that they are cheats, liars or thieves and while some managers may not believe they are, other managers surely will.

Let's think about some other questionable practices.

Why Do People Make Unethical Decisions?

What about your firm's time clock?
Have you ever seen one employee clock another in? 'Just doing 'em a favour' is the usual response when the offender is caught.

What about invoicing?
Have you ever experienced a time that your invoices were held for 60 days or 90 days without payment, because the company that owed you the money had a bit of a cash flow problem or wanted to earn the interest?

What about outside consultants?
Have you ever experienced having a consulting firm provide you with research findings and recommendations, only to learn that the consultants had not only faked the numbers but had also falsely recommended that you needed additional research to accomplish accurately what you wanted to know?

We are human

As young people we have our standards set for us by people we respect. Why, then, are these standards ignored later in life?

Why do people cut corners, or engage in shady behaviour, and yet choose not to see what they are doing in its true light? Why do some people expect to be excused for what they may think of as mere oversights when, in fact, these peccadilloes are actually unethical behaviour? Why does one manager see Mary's actions as acceptable and another say that what she did was wrong?

The answer is simple. It is because each of us is a unique individual, and each of us is human.

Each one of us is a complex combination of fears and doubts, of hopes and dreams, of dreads and worries. Each one of us is different. In fact, each one of us could be potential fodder for a Jeffrey Archer, Sidney Sheldon or Judith Krantz novel. Scratch the surface, and you can see that with a bit of creativity, each of our foibles or our aspirations might easily fit a character in *Eastenders*, *Coronation Street* or *The Bill*. In our own way, we are as idiosyncratic as those characters.

As people, each of us is a unique combination of our heredity, environment, abilities, talents and experiences. Just as we come to school or to marriage with those qualities, we come to the workplace with those strengths and weaknesses too; we come with talent. We come with 'baggage'. We come with needs, sensibilities, sensitivities, and values. We come with different kinds of education. Some lessons we learned at our mother's knee or by being bent over it, or we learned them on the playing field, in the classroom, in the church, synagogue or temple, or from the lollipop lady.

Just as we may have been born with blue eyes and brown hair to a particular set of parents in a particular location in the world — Kent, Singapore, San Antonio — we also have a personality that was both determined by birth and influenced by that environment.

What are the implications of those differences in the workplace?

Can you think of someone now in your employ who was the runt of the litter as a child, and, therefore, one who always had to struggle to be noticed? Was someone else the first-born and thus expected to be responsible for all his or her other siblings? How might those needs translate to the office? As a manager, you might well ask how you can be expected to know everything about the people you employ.

How can you know that an employee of yours was called a 'dosser' by a teacher and has been fighting to disassociate him or herself from that epithet for years?

How can you know that another employee may have been taught that asking for help is considered weak?

How can you know that another employee was an outstanding rugby player in school and became convinced that that athletic talent was the only quality that he had to offer?

Take a moment to reflect on some of your own sensitivities or self-doubts along with those of your staff. You, too, are different, are unique.

Why Do People Make Unethical Decisions?

As humans, we also dream. What of our hopes and aspirations? How do they translate to the office? What are some of your dreams?

You'll notice that I am not suggesting here that you write a list of your self-doubts, lest you leave this book at a meeting for everyone in the office to read!

But do answer the question: What are some of your dreams? You have talked to enough people socially across a restaurant table or formally across an interview desk to have heard all kinds of answers to that question about aspirations. In fact, don't we usually ask a form of that question in interviews? 'Where do you see yourself in x number of years?'

Our dreams are as varied as we are: to be loved, to be solvent, to have a 'Roller' or a 'Rover', a company car, a weekend home, money for college, Armani suits, a vacation in the south of France, time for ourselves, time to go fishing, to read, to write, to take a trip to Disney World, to win an award for 'BEST ...', to be famous, to earn political office, to have a corner office, to be married, to have more children, to retire young, to win the lottery, to go back to school, to get a degree.

Our dreams are indeed as individual as we are. And they are just that: dreams. Some are within our reach, others are not, but each of us has our share: 'I have always wanted to win Wimbledon, to be president, to be prime minister.' Although the dreams may change at different times in our lives, those hopes have a profound effect on us. In fact, they may drive us to behave in certain ways in different places, including the office.

In other words, even if we, as managers, see ourselves as hard-nosed business people, as task-oriented managers reading reports, analysing data, retrieving information, comparing statistics, studying forecasts, meeting clients, setting targets, we should be aware of ourselves. We should accept our own humanness. We should be equally aware of the humanness of people with whom we work: our superiors, our subordinates, our customers, our distributors, our loan officers or our board members.

It is all well and good to focus on completing the contract or finishing the report, meeting the deadline or distributing the product, but all of those activities involve human beings and human interactions, and that very humanness has profound implications for the way in which we do business. Our idiosyncrasies affect the way we do business. Our dreams affect the way we do business. Our values affect the way we do business. Our ethics affect the way we do business. And our dreams, values, idiosyncrasies and ethics affect the way people do business with us.

Motivation theories help us to understand ourselves

To assist us in analysing our own or our staff's behaviour, social scientists, psychologists and anthropologists have sought ways to help us understand ourselves. They have provided us with theories and hypotheses to use as measuring sticks. These theories are not absolute laws nor do they provide us with hard data about why we do what we do or what percentage of our behaviour is based on heredity, or how birth order or childhood nutrition affect our emotional make-up. However, they do provide insights and recommendations for our consideration.

For example, many social scientists have tried to help us know ourselves and each other by developing and testing theories which attempt to give us information about what drives us.

Abraham Maslow
Years ago, motivation theorist, Abraham Maslow, offered us his hierarchy of needs, that now famous pyramid by which he

Why Do People Make Unethical Decisions?

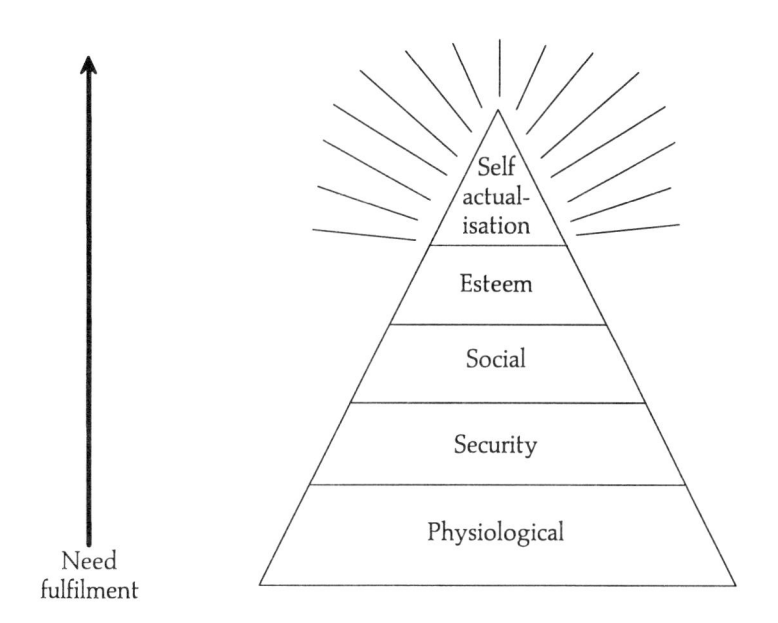

```
↑                    Self
|                 actualisation
|                  _____
|                 /   Esteem   \
|                /_____\
|               /    Social      \
|              /_____\
|             /     Security       \
|            /_____\
|           /      Physiological     \
|          /_____\
Need
fulfilment
```

sought to help us visualise our needs. He perceived each of us
Maslow's hierarchy of needs

as moving, over time, from the bottom of the pyramid to the top.

When we are at the bottom, we need food for survival. Then, having eaten, we seek shelter from the elements for our safety and security. Then he suggested that once we are fed and safe, humans seek relationships with others. He went on to say that once those basic needs are met, we shift our focus to more emotional ones, those concerned with our self-esteem and our self-actualisation. In other words, we need recognition.

Although some scholars now view Maslow's approach as dated, the pyramid or hierarchy is still a useful way to visualise our needs. Most of us can relate to the notion of needing a crust of bread to eat and a roof over our heads. At that level of need we might say, 'I'll do anything. I just need a job.' In that instance, what is a job? It's a means of keeping the wolf from the door.

But stay for a moment with Maslow's theory. Those of us

for whom getting, keeping and changing jobs is not an issue, or at least hasn't been for some time, may see ourselves as higher on the pyramid. We are more concerned with working conditions, with how we are treated, with how we are paid for what we do. In our first jobs our concern may have been that we were simply being paid. We could afford our first flat or a weekend away.

Consistent with Maslow's model, there are those of us who ultimately reach the point when we might be able to say, 'Yes, I can make my mortgage payments; my boss is a decent person, but this job just isn't me. I need to feel good about myself, and somehow doing what I am currently doing just isn't very satisfying any more.' That kind of need would be consistent with Maslow's notion of self-actualisation, which suggests that we have an on-going need for personal development and growth, to feel good about ourselves.

Clayton Alderfer

Maslow is only one of many theorists who have tried to develop means for us to examine ourselves and each other from the context of our needs and our drives. Another theorist, Clayton Alderfer, hypothesised that we don't always move up the hierarchy, that we can move down as well as up, thus suggesting that our needs change as our circumstances change.

David C McClelland

Yet another scholar, McClelland, used other descriptors in his analysis of our behaviour at work. He suggested that some of us are motivated by challenge, by achievement, that still others among us are motivated to be collegial. Having good working relationships is important to us. He labelled that drive as affiliation. Others among us, he said, may be driven by a need for power.

From his perspective, using his notions, we can ask ourselves to consider whether or not we are driven to overcome obstacles, to climb the mountain, because it is there, or better yet, to create a mountain so that we can climb it. Or

Why Do People Make Unethical Decisions?

we can consider if we are the kind of people for whom it is more important to have colleagues at work with whom we can relate or who respect us, than it is to overcome obstacles. Others of us may be motivated by the need for power. Do we feel frustrated, if, in fact, someone else has the final impact on the decision-making? Again, do you see some of your work colleagues in this model?

Locus of control

One useful theoretical construct relates to our perception of what controls our lives. It is yet another variable in our make-up. Theorists have offered us the notion of 'locus of control'. By this is meant that we can categorise people as falling into one of two large groups: those who feel that they have significant control over their own lives and work and those who feel that they have little control over what happens to them. If you had to put yourself in one or the other category, where might you be?

_____

_____

_____

Where would your staff be?

_____

_____

_____

There are still other theories, more recent than those of Maslow and Alderfer, that offer a more dynamic model of what we do and why we do it. These are the expectancy theories, in which our outputs are shown to reflect dynamic inputs. These theories ask us to examine the interplay between our expectations and the rewards which affect our performance. For example, if Norman frequently represents Lisa's work as his own, as he did earlier, how might Lisa's performance be affected by his actions?

Regardless of whether or not you are familiar with, accept or apply a particular theory or know the writings of certain people, such as Maslow, Alderfer, McClelland or others, their work reminds us that theorists have sought to help us come to terms with the fact that each of us is a complex creature who is motivated by diverse needs and drives. That is true of the people you manage. It is true of the person who manages you. It is true of you.

Applying theories helps us to understand ourselves

Let us return to the issue of why people make unethical decisions and try to understand how that question can be related to what we've just been discussing. Yes, we are reared with a set of values given to us by diverse people, and, yes, we are all idiosyncratic, with dreams and aspirations that vary with each of us.

In addition, each of us is a complex bundle of standards and dreams, of doubts and convictions. We also have varying motivations and needs at different times in our lives. Given the combination of what each of us wants and what is important to us, given what drives us and what we value, you can see that at any time each of us may behave in ways that enable us to best achieve what we want and need.

Pressures may cause us to act unethically

Diverse influences may affect our ethics. What we want or need may outweigh our considerations of right and wrong. As a result, personal pressures may put our needs above those of others. Sometimes those pressures are such that we behave unethically.

- Remember Norman. Maybe, it is important to Norman to please his boss because he wants the recognition that will follow. Maybe the pressure is such that he will pass off Lisa's work as his own in an effort to be publicly or

privately lauded by his supervisor.
- Meet Phyllis. Maybe that Roller, Rover or larger office is so important to her sense of self that she is prepared to cut a few corners, or make a few shady deals to ensure that she achieves quota.
- Meet Tim. Maybe having perceived himself as a failure in some other aspect of his life, Tim will do anything to ensure that his division is seen as the most successful in the organisation.
- Meet Peggy. Maybe her need to amass power or to win drives her to disregard the colleagues she hurts on the way up the corporate ladder. That pressure to win may outweigh any earlier training in which she was taught not to do harm to others.
- Meet Cory. This young man has learned to rationalise what he does. His need is to be liked by others. He does not behave with integrity, because it is easier for him to hide the truth and to agree with everyone. He believes that being a 'yes' man might enhance his opportunities to be well thought of.
- Meet Shirley. She wants to demonstrate to management what an intelligent businessperson she is, so she saves a few pennies by using inferior materials in the product.

In many cases, our own lack of insight into ourselves, into others, into what drives us as individuals or motivates us as managers and supervisors causes us to dismiss our humanness as inconsequential. We have weaknesses; we are jealous; we get angry; we seek revenge; we worry; we bear grudges; we behave unethically. Sometimes we forget those realities when we go to work.

We forget to think about values

Although a few people may be motivated by some Machiavellian need for power over others and might deliberately go to extreme lengths to achieve their ends, when it comes to making unethical decisions the reason, more often than not, is that we just don't think about the ethics of the situation. We are so focused on getting the job done that we don't take time to reflect on the values involved in the situation.

It is not that Mary is a bad person for wanting to phone her Mum or her sister. As a matter of fact, she may be a very caring person. Her need was to find out about the well-being of her family. She probably didn't even think about the ethical implications of using the company telephone. But then, perhaps no one asked her to think about it.

Surely, Norman didn't make a conscious decision to pass off Lisa's work as his own. He just wanted to do well and get the job done. So he probably didn't think about how Lisa or anyone else might view his passing her work off as his own.

If Cory knew that there was some organisational problem, maybe he felt that it was simply the wisest decision to say nothing rather than upset his colleagues and risk their being angry with him. Perhaps he assumed that they must know what they are doing. He may not have thought of who else might get hurt by his silence.

Acts reflecting a lack of concern for values are not necessarily conspiratorial, despite media suggestions to the contrary. Whatever our motivation, we often make decisions that are strictly bottom line. Those choices are hastily made, and the implications of who is affected or who might get hurt, or whether or not there were other choices available to us at the time, are completely overlooked.

Insight is often based on hindsight

There are classic cases of insight based on hindsight, of short-term versus long-term thinking. For example, Ford executives decided not to make a change in the design of the Pinto automobile because of the significant cost that the change would entail. In retrospect, they might have invested the $11 per vehicle if they had anticipated the cost to the company in human lives and in litigation.

The engineers and management involved in the tragic Challenger explosion learned the error of their thinking when they let external pressures affect their decision to launch despite their knowledge of a possible design flaw. Today, when there is doubt about the space shuttle, launches are postponed.

Therefore, as managers, we should bear in mind that we are all brought up with standards, that we are all unique and are motivated by different needs and drives. As managers, we should think about ourselves and our subordinates as people with strengths and weaknesses. As managers, we should ensure that our staff are encouraged to reflect on themselves, on what they are doing, on why they are doing it, as well as on what they may be forgetting to do in their rush to get the job done.

Whether it's Norman passing off Lisa's work, Cory saying 'yes' when he should say 'wait' or NASA launching a rocket without heeding the engineers' warning, that short-term solution may have lasting consequences. Simply, if unethical events happen wittingly or unwittingly in our business relationships, whether between ourselves and our colleagues or between ourselves and the public, there are serious implications for those errors or oversights. Let's look at some of those costs.

CHAPTER 3
What Does Unethical Behaviour Cost?

Chapter 1 referred to a short list of some familiar names that have become increasingly better known for reasons other than the quality of their products and services. Union Carbide, BCCI, Michael Miliken and Nestlé were included; you may have added a few more. In fact, these names represent only a fraction of the people and organisations that have been in the news because of questionable dealings in some grey, undefined, perhaps unregulated area of business.

Some say that there are no costs to unethical behaviour

You could compile another kind of list, but you would have more difficulty doing so, because no newspapers or TV headlines would help you to identify who these individuals are or where to locate the firms. This second list entitled, 'The Ones Who Pulled it Off,' would include the names of people, firms, corporations, partnerships, one person offices, and/or individuals who have employed fraudulent practices for years and who have never been caught.

You will undoubtedly meet or work with people who will reject any discussion of ethics. And why? First, they will fail to see the merit in the positive implications of the issue and second, they won't see the costs associated with unethical practices.

Therefore, before analysing the costs to you and your organisation that may be associated with unethical behaviour as well as the potential benefits of being ethical, it's important to recognise that there are those who would argue against the practicality of being ethical in business.

One reason for that view is that the outcomes of shady dealings are not all negative. To the contrary, some business people are successful at making money that way; why else would they embark on such courses of action?

Despite the view that suggests there is no need to address ethics, increasing numbers of managers are becoming aware that more companies or individuals are 'getting caught', that politicians are resigning, or that even major athletes are being sidelined because of questionable practices. Of course, not everyone is caught, resigns or is sidelined. Charlatans have had successful careers. Many business people have become 'rich quick' on the gullibility or dreams of other people.

This is not intended to suggest that business people are inherently dishonest. Certainly not. But there are many business people who have been behaving unethically because they look about them and see how many have been getting away with such behaviour for years. And they are often not reluctant to cite examples of nefarious behaviour leading to success: 'I know someone who has been doing thus and so, living the high life in the south of somewhere.'

Crimes go unsolved, and criminals get away with murder, despite the efforts of Morse or Wexford or even the police. In the same way, those who succeed in business by employing unethical practices may 'get away with it' as well.

But are there no costs whatsoever?

There are costs associated with success through deception. Expenditure of energy might be one. Imagine investing precious resources to ensure that your questionable practices don't become too public, that you don't get caught, or that

What Does Unethical Behaviour Cost?

you don't become prey to blackmailers. Picture such an individual needing two sets of books, hiding accounts in false bottom drawers or on exotic islands, ensuring that no one sees certain papers or overhears phone conversations. It must be wearying to swear people to secrecy. It must be tiresome to hope that the Inland Revenue won't notice, that customers overlooked the bad fruit, the slightly damaged products or the inflated prices. It must be draining to anticipate a problem and then have to script a way out of it.

If you have ever met people who do business 'on the edge', can you recall an incident involving them? Were there costs that you noticed?

This description of such manoeuvring is reminiscent of the plots of B films, the characters in Elmore Leonard novels or scenes from sixteenth-century farces or Keystone Cop films, with people running in and out of doorways chased madly by the police. Although motivation theory suggests there are those who thrive on challenge, for most, a life of deception can hardly be the preferred option.

Maybe we would deceive, if we were better at it

Perhaps we would be out there living a life of constant deceit, if we were better liars. Without labouring the point about the costs of living deceitfully, can you recall an incident from your childhood, at home or in school, when you resorted to lying as a defence? Perhaps you received a mark in class that you knew would disappoint your parents. Perhaps you played truant from school. Recall such an incident:

_____

_____

_____

_____

I remember skipping class. Within minutes of doing so I met a relative on the street. I felt so guilty that even without being asked why I wasn't in class, I blustered my way, offering some lame excuse. Later, after having been found out by Mum and Dad, I took one last shot at getting out of my predicament. When asked what I had been doing, where I had been going and then why I had done what I had done, I lied again. I think it was Dad who said, 'I can always tell when you are lying. Look me in the eye.'

I kept the lie going. It is said that the secret of good lying is to be vague. But I wasn't vague enough. I dug a deeper and deeper hole for myself, because I provided details which were inconsistent with the rest of my pathetic fiction. The scenario didn't ring true. I was a poor liar, and I was punished.

Other school mates were more proficient at lying than I was: those who didn't do their homework and got away with it, who cheated on exams and got away with it, who told fibs and got away with it.

There are costs to being deceitful

Fun though it may be to reflect on some childhood pranks and to recall that there are those who were successful deceivers and those who weren't, remember what is really at issue here: that just as we paid for our indiscretions years ago with reprimands, punishments or temporary banishments to our rooms, there are costs associated with unethical behaviour in business. These costs have the potential to be far more damaging than being denied the use of the car for the week, going to bed without supper or having to write on the board 100 times our promise not to repeat our misdemeanour.

The costs of being unethical in business are significant

Ethics may appear to be a subject that is soft and intangible. However, in the final analysis, the lack of ethics may damage what is hard, tangible and measurable, the bottom line, the dollars and cents, the pounds and pence. In addition,

What Does Unethical Behaviour Cost?

reputation and career may be ruined because ethics is ignored.

Loss of trust

Your success as a manager is, in part, contingent on your ability to establish trust. Consider the sequence of events involving two people, Sally and John. Notice how the loss of that trust might lead to loss of confidentiality, to censored communication, to poor self-esteem, to lack of commitment, to diminished loyalty and, ultimately, to resignation. With the exception of the last, resignation, each one of these words represents an intangible element which is essential to your success as you establish and maintain business relationships.

But before looking at the scenario, bear in mind this basic assumption: successful business relationships are built on the conviction that each party believes that what the other person is saying is true. For example:

- You accept a supplier's promise to deliver a product to you within a specific time frame. The supplier expects to be paid in a timely fashion.
- You agree to the charges for research set by a consultant. The consultant assumes that those are the fees that will be paid.
- You delegate tasks on the basis that the person you instructed to do them will complete them. The individual believes that those are the tasks and the time frame that you require.
- You employ people and count on their commitment to do the job well. Those individuals expect that the promises made when they were hired will be honoured.

Can you identify other instances in which trust is inherent in a business relationship?

_____

_____

_____

Business Ethics

Consider what the consequences are for those relationships, if there is no trust between yourself and the other party.

Recall a situation in which you lost your confidence in a client, a subordinate, a superior, a supplier or a board member:

_____
_____
_____
_____

What incident or action prompted you to lose faith in that person or in the firm you were dealing with?

- [ ] Was it the product?
- [ ] Was it the service?
- [ ] Was it the accounting procedures?
- [ ] Was it the staff?
- [ ] Was it personal behaviour?
- [ ] Was it something else? _____

_____
_____
_____

Or did all these elements combine, so that you simply didn't trust an individual's word?   Yes ☐   No ☐

How did that loss of trust affect your ongoing relationship with that individual or with that company?

_____
_____
_____
_____
_____

What Does Unethical Behaviour Cost?

Are you still doing business with that person or company? If you are, why? If you are not, why not?

_____

_____

_____

However you described your own experience, if you reflect on what happened, you should recognise that one of the costs associated with unethical behaviour is loss of trust.

Perhaps you recalled a situation in which promises were not kept or contracts were not honoured. You may have identified a situation in which you were misled. At first, as many of us would, you decided to give the individuals involved the benefit of the doubt. But, if the same situation happened again and again, you probably lost confidence and faith in those who made the promises and who then failed to honour their commitments.

That person will have lost credibility. When that happens, you will probably do business elsewhere.

Loss of one's good name
Another cost associated with unethical behaviours or practices resulting from the loss of trust may be one's good name. Research tells us that unhappy consumers tell more people about bad service than they do about good service. In that very way, a fine reputation can be replaced with a poor one. A company previously known for its good name can quickly become infamous for double-dealing, for promises not kept or for employing other shoddy business practices.

What are some internal consequences once trust is lost?

Less effective teamwork
To begin our scenario, let's look at one important organisational requirement, teamwork, and decide what happens to

goals, tasks or projects when there is no trust among the members of a team. Sally is a colleague of John. We'll focus on John. Bear in mind that Sally is the villain of the piece and that her behaviour goes unchecked.

They have worked in the same company for some time. Until recently John trusted her, but several recent incidents have occurred causing John to be uneasy about Sally. He is beginning to sense that she needs to feed her ambition. She wants money, power and advancement. And John suspects that she might go to any lengths to get what she wants.

In what ways might those doubts about Sally affect their relationship if they were assigned to work together on a team?

_____

_____

_____

_____

You may have listed any number of concerns about the effectiveness of their working relationship. Ultimately, John will have difficulty doing his job. How can they function together if she sees John as a threat to her advancement, or if John is not sure of her motivation? Will she be fair? John will wonder. Will she manipulate information? Will she try to manipulate him? Will John wonder whether or not he should be involved in this project at all? Might he try to get off the team? Will he start second guessing what she meant by what she just said? Might he wonder whether or not he should share his ideas with her, suspecting that she might use them for her own personal advantage?

Those are possible downsides of John's diminishing trust in Sally. As a manager, you can see what might happen to any team that you create if there is a lack of trust among the members. Individuals may hold back, may not be available for meetings, may not take risks or offer creative solutions.

What Does Unethical Behaviour Cost?

In what other ways might the loss of trust among team members impact your department or your company?

_____

_____

_____

_____

Loss of confidentiality
If John doesn't trust Sally's motives and, therefore, Sally herself, perhaps he'll wonder what she'll do with any and all information, not just what she receives from the team. Perhaps it is her lack of confidentiality that concerns him. If a member of the team openly makes a disparaging remark about a company policy or about the value of the project that they are undertaking, where will that information go? Will John find himself wondering how he can share any confidential information about another employee with Sally, for example, about a current bargaining position with the union, about a client or about the subject of a takeover? Can he trust her with a critical item of proprietary information that might be valuable to another organisation? Considering her ambition, he might wonder to whom she might give that information.

A decline in the sharing of confidential information, both positive and negative, is likely. If John doesn't know what Sally will do with what he has told her, how can he risk sharing that data with her or letting her attend a meeting that he is calling at which sensitive matters are discussed?

Censored communication
As the trust diminishes, as confidentiality wanes, what happens to communication, a vital component in the health of an organisation? If John no longer trusts his relationship with Sally, he will probably no longer trust her work, her calculations. He will no longer have faith that she will do the job that needs to be done. Sally's reputation will continue to fall in John's eyes. Perhaps he thinks that she has revealed

Business Ethics

information about a new budget line that was under consideration to a member of another department. Or he is convinced that she carried tales to senior management that came from a team meeting – all for the purpose of enhancing her position and thus her own growth.

How can he continue to communicate with her about any topic in the same way? Certainly, he is prepared to make small talk, or to relay messages, but it is also likely that he will censor all of his conversations with her, withholding any kind of feedback, wondering what she will do with any titbit of information.

> Stop for a moment. Let's alter the scenario and make the situation even worse. Imagine that the person who cannot be trusted, Sally, is your boss, and that *you* are John. What are the implications for that relationship?
>
> _____
>
> _____
>
> _____
>
> _____

But, let's return to the less unpleasant original scenario in which Sally and John are colleagues. If, as we said, Sally misuses or distorts information, it won't be long before John won't provide any information at all. If John hears *his* ideas spewing forth from Sally as if they were her own, how long will it be before he stops sharing any and all of his ideas with her?

Loss of self-esteem

So far what has happened? John's distrust of his former colleague, Sally, has increased. He has lost faith in her

What Does Unethical Behaviour Cost?

confidentiality. Their communication has decreased as well. As communication declines, a willingness to share ideas or to take risks also decreases. If the theorists are remotely accurate in their analysis of human nature, it is more than likely that the next loss may be related to John's sense of self.

Why? Most of us respond in the same way when we see confidentiality violated. Our first instinct is to kick ourselves for not seeing the obvious and then to ask ourselves why we trusted that person in the first place. John, too, may ask himself why he didn't see it coming. Why didn't he recognise what was happening?

When someone we trusted breaks confidentiality or neglects responsibility, typically the first person that we find fault with is ourself. Sure, we get angry at the other person. As managers, we may counsel or discipline the individual for the breach, but we also tend to blame our own judgement for failing to see the handwriting on the wall. We ask ourselves questions like: Why did we hire that individual? Why didn't we supervise him or her better? Why did we give him that project when he couldn't handle it? Why did we let her negotiate with a client?

Thus, we may begin to doubt our own judgement.

In John's case, maybe he allows that self-doubt to affect his other areas of responsibility. Maybe he'll rethink the effectiveness of his new approach to hiring; perhaps he is no longer sure that his approach is such a good idea. Maybe he loses confidence in a proposal that he is working on, or begins to second guess or censor his own ideas. Despite all the books and courses on the power of positive thinking that are published, humans are highly self-critical. And his relationship with Sally may reinforce his doubts and insecurities.

Lack of commitment

If his self-esteem is damaged and John becomes unsure about the efficacy of his actions or the wisdom of his ideas, it might not be surprising for his enthusiasm for the position and for the company to wane.

Business Ethics

Once again, let's alter the situation. Suppose John's frustration is not only related to his relationship with his colleague, Sally, but also with his boss and with the way that deals are done in the company. Studies have shown that organisations under attack because of a takeover threat or because of highly publicised litigation experience a decline in employee morale. In such situations, it is not surprising that employees lose confidence in the company and in themselves. Therefore another cost, when employees lose confidence in the way business is transacted, is a loss of commitment. John has lost his.

In other words, John and Sally as members of a team do not trust each other. If a team's energy is being expended on protecting flanks from attacks by colleagues or from upper management, then it shouldn't be long before the desire to perform well for the success of the company will fade. In John's case, he might begin to ask: What is the point in trying to succeed in this company, to having an innovative solution to a problem, to staying late to assist a colleague with a knotty problem, when none of these actions is valued or when there is no trust?

Declining loyalty

Loyalty goes hand in hand with commitment, to say nothing of responsibility. How do you recognise the disaffected employee?

_____

_____

_____

_____

Listen to John at closing time as a customer with a problem seeks service: 'Someone else can handle this, not me. My job is over at five, so it's not my problem.'

Listen to the employee who has an innovative solution to a problem: 'Why should I share this idea with management?

What Does Unethical Behaviour Cost?

Someone else will just take credit for it without acknowledging my initiative.'

Listen to the employee who used to be eager to learn: 'Why should I make an effort to read or take courses or seek greater responsibility when jobs are handed out through favouritism, nepotism or bribery?'

Listen to all of these people: 'If the company is giving nothing back to me, why should I give it my loyalty?'

Resignation

As a manager, you might say that someone with this level of demotivation should go and good riddance. In fact, it will not be long before the disaffected employee opens the newspapers to the classified adverts. If it is John, he will be heard moaning over a coffee or a brew about how badly business is conducted. There will be endless monologues about the pointlessness of making a commitment to such a poorly managed company. Those same whines and moans will undoubtedly be shared over the telephone with customers or prospective clients. Coffee breaks will become whinging sessions.

Sooner or later, such an unhappy employee is sure to retire from the job or opt to leave the organisation in search of greener, fairer pastures. On the one hand, you could be left with the cost of recruitment, induction and training of a new employee and the possible need to double up responsibilities while the position is vacant. On the other hand, if it is John, and he doesn't leave, you will find yourself concerned about the messages and attitudes he is conveying to other members of the department. In either event, quality of service is likely to decline.

Let's keep going with this grim scenario. Should such employees opt to leave, they may have difficulty finding new jobs. How demoralised will such employees be? Will it show up in the screening process? How nervous will they be about making another mistake in their choice of employer? Unethical experiences early in someone's career can colour their future interactions. Has it happened to you?

Books are written about the implications of a failed marriage on an individual's self-esteem. How many are written about the damage done to self-esteem from the failure of another significant contract, the one between employers and their employees? Newly divorced or separated people are said to have difficulty trusting their judgements and to be nervous about committing to new relationships. That same insecurity can be true in business relationships. We have all heard someone say, 'I never want to work with someone like that again!'

Trust matters

The preceding scenario with Sally and John is negative and simplistic, but it is also possible. It describes a steady decline in an individual's ability to perform, one that offers little hope of redemption. You might well say that John is overreacting and that the problem is being blamed on one individual's values and unethical behaviour. Certainly, other factors also affect performance. Some employees are inherently lazy, are not skilled or are unwilling or unable to learn, or they enjoy camaraderie more than they do work. However, more often than not, most employees thrive on positive aspects of work: growth, trust and responsibility.

Underline that point about trust and responsibility. Imagine how you would feel if a manager said to you, 'Please write a progress report for Thursday's meeting.' How would you feel if another manager barked, 'Draft a report and be sure that I see it to check that you haven't left anything out.' Wouldn't you prefer to work for the manager who believes in your ability to do the job?

It is difficult to have pride in your own work if you are given no responsibility or are not trusted to be committed to doing a job well. Recall an experience when someone trusted you to get the job done rather than double-checked your every move:

What Does Unethical Behaviour Cost?

_____
_____
_____

How did that trust affect your working style and level of commitment?

_____
_____
_____

Once again, let's pose the question of the cost of unethical behaviour. Having considered the extreme scenario of Sally and John, you can see that on a personal level an individual may be devastated. As you did earlier, multiply that individual's reaction by several more people in a department or by several departments. If you do, you can see how that initial loss of trust might change attitude, which in turn might impact creativity, productivity, motivation or performance.

But what about the cost of unethical behaviour to an organisation itself?

Let's look at some macro issues. Instead of examining the impact on an individual working in an uncomfortable, unethical environment, let's look at the possible impact of unethical practices on the organisation as a whole. By thinking of some actual companies, you are already aware of what has been the price of unethical behaviour when that behaviour has become public knowledge.

There is no doubt that major corporations or business moguls of the world have paid mightily when their nefarious conduct was revealed. We know that in extreme cases some individuals have been imprisoned. Others may have chosen suicide, rather than face the public humiliation that such scrutiny leads to. Others have forfeited their careers. The families of such individuals have suffered too. Flight, public scrutiny and imprisonment have affected not only the individual but also his or her family.

The consequences are not always that dire or sinister. Individual managers in companies have paid for their own and their company's errors. They have paid for the lessons that they learned. Some have been sacked, others have been fined, still others have had their roles in the company changed or have been relocated to different branches. Some have been suspended with pay and some without. In other words, individual companies usually have established a range of punishments to mete out when unethical practices are uncovered.

Damage to a company name or the suggestion of impropriety may lead to a fall-off in sales. A referral may opt to do business elsewhere, orders may decline. Ultimately, so will the profits. Questions will be asked: Is the product or service untrustworthy? Has there been mishandling of public monies and public trust? Does the product do what the consumer expects it to do, or is it going to cause injury? Might the product burst into flame or poison the user? Did the product carry a warning on the label? Did the company know that the product was flawed or defective before it was ordered or purchased?

What are likely implications of unethical conduct? Litigation, for one. If that's the case, lawyers and barristers cost money. Trials cost money, so do in and out of court settlements. Legal paperwork is expensive. Where is that money coming from? To what project was it allocated, and how will it now be used instead? Will redesign, refurbishment or essential new development be put on hold? It is not just the cost of lawyers that must be calculated. What about that now-tarnished image?

What have companies done to redeem their good names?

You have seen what companies have done: the ad campaigns that apologise, that explain, the press conferences that justify,

What Does Unethical Behaviour Cost?

and the redesigned package or product. What about the corporate videos, the new logos? Some companies have given themselves a facelift in order to regain market share. In the same way that significant sums may have to be spent on unexpected legal problems, some companies have found it essential to spend significant monies on new layouts, designs, spin doctors, or public relations firms, in an effort to renew the public's faith in the way that they do business. This is done in an effort to regain public confidence and public trust.

To borrow someone else's analogy, it is difficult to drive full speed ahead with your eyes on the rear-view mirror. An organisation that is dealing with the burden of the public awareness of unethical dealings cannot be focusing on the road ahead, on its mission and objectives, on who or what is gaining on it, or even passing. Instead, such an organisation is expending resources working out where it has been and on how it got there. That rearward-looking behaviour is a consequence of unethical practice. Given these individual and organisational costs, given the desire for a manager to be proactive rather than reactive, what might you as a manager do to create an ethical working environment?

CHAPTER 4
How Can You Create an Ethical Working Environment?

Since there are significant downsides to being unethical or to working in an unethical environment, you might well wonder what you, as an individual manager, can do to foster an ethical working environment. The fact is that you can do a great deal for yourself, your staff, your organisation and your stakeholders by considering and implementing the following eight steps:

Step 1: Make the decision to commit to ethics
Step 2: Recognise that you are a role model by definition, by your actions and by your values
Step 3: Assume the responsibility for instilling ethical behaviour
Step 4: Determine what you consider to be ethical practice
Step 5: Articulate your values
Step 6: Train your staff
Step 7: Encourage open communication
Step 8: Be consistent.

Step 1. Make the decision to commit to ethics

The first step in the process requires that you make a decision that ethics is important to your firm's success and to your own personal success in business. If you decide that ethics is important, you should be prepared to invest resources which will support your commitment to foster an ethical climate. When you make that investment, you will see that most of those resources will involve allocating time to ethics. At a later stage, your staff's time will be needed too.

If you are prepared to accept and commit to the importance of ethics, then you should put your concern for values on to your list of priorities. For many, ethics will be a new item, and people will wonder why you are expending so much time thinking and talking about it. For others, if values are already on your priority list, then you may want to move them higher. In other words, ethics should become an agenda item in the same way that new technologies, staffing or budgetary concerns are. Bear in mind that most agenda items involve the allocation of resources. Business ethics is no less important an item and deserves no less an acknowledgement of commitment.

Before you involve any of your staff in the process of value setting, you will need to reflect again on some of your own experiences. Once you have decided that the inclusion of ethics in decision-making is important in the process of creating an ethical working environment, and once you are prepared to commit to addressing the issue, then the second step is for you to take a hard look at yourself as a manager, to recognise what a significant role model you are for the people with whom you interact.

Step 2. Recognise that you are a role model by definition, by your actions and by your values

Role model by definition
Sometimes it is difficult for you as a manager, particularly if

How Can You Create an Ethical Working Environment?

you are new to the position, to realise that by definition you are a role model. Even if you've been doing the job for a while, you can forget the enormity of your impact on other people. It becomes easy to take for granted that you have power, that you have influence, that you set standards simply by being the manager.

So remind yourself that you have that power because you have been given a job with specific responsibilities or functions. You have a title, be it supervisor, manager or director. Your relationships with the people with whom you do business — subordinates, customers, MD — are affected by that role, by that title and by the decisions that you make in that capacity. *You* call the meetings; *you* decide who will or will not attend. *You* set the agenda.

Let's make the concept of role model clearer by having you think about your relationship with your own boss. How are you affected by his or her presence, requests or attitudes? Are you aware that his or her standards and expectations affect your sense of responsibility for doing the job that he or she expects of you? The importance of your boss may be manifested in the urgency and quality of the reports you write, how you manage the division, or your commitment to increased profitability. Given your duties, your own focus may be on living up to the expectations of those individuals who identified you as the ideal candidate for the job. So, you are determined to complete the tasks and assume the responsibilities that have been laid out for you by those in command.

Now turn the situation around. You are the boss. Your subordinates react to you in the same way that you react to your superiors.

What are some of your current key tasks and responsibilities?

_____

_____

_____

Did you include any reference to setting standards for others?

Yes ☐   No ☐

If you did include setting standards for others, then you have already taken that essential second step, which is to recognise that you are a role model. If you did not write anything about standards or values setting, perhaps you are minimising, forgetting, or not realising your impact on others.

Some people find it easier to notice that effect on others than on themselves, particularly if they are in their current position because they were promoted internally. If *you* were, think back to the days when your promotion was announced and you took over the position. Shortly thereafter you may have noticed that colleagues with whom you previously had lunch or coffee began to behave differently in your presence. You had changed.

If that was your experience, what did you notice?

_____

_____

_____

Perhaps the change took the form of greater formality in your relationships. Perhaps the tone or the subject of a conversation altered when you approached the lunch table or when you neared a group of people who were talking. Although you believed that you were exactly the same person that you were before promotion, the reality is that, by definition, you had changed.

As a manager it's important to accept the fact that in other people's eyes, you, along with your job and your title, have changed.

If you still need convincing about the number of changes that may have occurred, think of some of the physical ones. For example, do you have your own office or a larger one, or

How Can You Create an Ethical Working Environment?

an office in a more desirable location in the building? Is the furniture more impressive, or is your name now on the door, whereas it was not before? Perhaps you have a PA or a secretary, when previously no such support was available to you. Now you have a private line and a cellular phone. You are expected to attend meetings that once you were not privy to. Maybe your name is now on a different, more prestigious distribution list.

Those changes could have come automatically with the promotion, but it is possible that you decided to make some of your own. What changes did you make when you assumed a managerial role for the first time?

_____

_____

_____

What did you include in your list of changes? Did you indicate that you:

- ☐ changed your style of clothing?
- ☐ wear suits more often than you did before?
- ☐ wear more conservative colours?
- ☐ have a hairstyle more appropriate for your new role?
- ☐ gave up using your nickname?
- ☐ asked your secretary to answer the phone formally?
- ☐ purchased a new briefcase?
- ☐ selected different pictures for your office?
- ☐ and: _____

_____

_____

In sum, once you are in a management role, whether by internal promotion or external selection, there are changes. These changes are because of the job title itself, the nature of the job, because of what you do and because of what others perceive you as doing. But the nature of your decisions alters as well.

Role model by action
Management is about decision-making. Regardless of your specific job title or area of responsibility, many of the decisions that you make are about the people with whom you interact, the people you manage or supervise. Specifically, in your capacity:

- You will find that you have the responsibility for evaluating other people's work.
- You will be selecting people to handle particular projects based on your evaluation of their skills and abilities.
- You will be identifying individuals for promotion, for awards, for special taskforces or teams.
- You will be granting or denying special requests, such as for an afternoon off to see the dentist.
- You will be identifying who should take a leadership role at a team meeting.
- You will be relieving someone of current duties in order to serve on a select committee.
- You will be considering a staff member for specialised training.

You are now the boss. Your subordinates know that your evaluation, your appraisal, affects their careers as well as their pay packets. In essence, your staff knows without being told that you are influential. Therefore, they know that to succeed they will have to meet with your approval and your expectations. As a manager, you cannot afford to forget that you are being watched and scrutinised. The physical trappings of the role will be noticed: the polished shoes, the quality hair cut, the style of the clothes, the condition of the office as well as the amount of paperwork on the desk.

Role model by your values
To foster the growth of an ethical environment, you have to

How Can You Create an Ethical Working Environment?

accept that you are a role model, not only because of your choice of clothing and your office layout, but also because of your values. Your attitudes, decisions, practices, and your behaviour are scrutinised and, in many cases, replicated by those who report to you.

Again, think about your own experience with a boss that you may have reported to sometime in your career. What were some of the positive or negative actions or attitudes of that individual which might have become a standard for you or for your colleagues?

_____

_____

_____

_____

Did you have bosses who arrived late to work every day?
Were they the last in and the first out?
Did they set meetings for 10:00, but then arrive at 10:30?
Did they promise to return phone calls before Friday, but failed to do so until the following Tuesday?
Did most of his or her phone calls begin with, 'Sorry, I couldn't get back to you sooner, but ...'?
Did they publicly humiliate subordinates?
Were they always in a hurry?
Were they disorganised?
Did they have an agenda for meetings?
Did they plan ahead?
Did they clearly and patiently explain what they wanted from people?
Were they rude and abrupt?
Did they play favourites?
Did they treat subordinates with contempt?
Were they incapable of making a decision without calling a meeting?
Were they bullies?
Did they treat people from different backgrounds differently?

Business Ethics

Did they listen?
Were they patient?
Were they approachable?
Were they honest?
Did they tell you one thing and do another?
Did they knowingly harm someone?
Were they unfair?
Did they honour confidentiality?
Were they trusted?
Did they make thoughtful, long-term decisions or only short-term, expedient ones?

Every item on this list, and more besides, sets the standards that you and your colleagues worked by.

Now look back at that same list and ask yourself how you compare. What standards are you setting for your staff?

To create an ethical environment, it is important not to underestimate how visible some of your unspoken values may be. Like your speech pattern or phone manner, your standards affect the people with whom you come in contact. You are training your staff in your way of doing business, soundlessly, without articulating your standards. Thus, if you are rude and abrasive on the phone when you are under pressure, then it is easy for a member of your staff to model that behaviour. The lesson to be learned is that if the boss does it, so can I. In essence, without even calling a meeting to articulate your rules, standards, or values, what you do and how you behave reflect your inner values.

So, don't minimise the impact that you have on those with whom you work. Just as an employee will compliment you on

How Can You Create an Ethical Working Environment?

your new haircut or new optical frames, other less tangible details will be noted as well.

> Some years ago a young man I know was appointed to a senior management position in an organisation with a limited budget. Within weeks of his appointment, the architects and builders were breaking down walls to enlarge his office. New carpeting, curtains and furniture were selected, walls were repainted and the latest computers and technology installed. Within a few more weeks of his appointment, and in spite of the fact that his staff consisted of both men and women, he handed out plum jobs to the men, particularly to officers in the union. What values do you think he was communicating to his staff?
>
> _____
>
> _____
>
> _____
>
> How do you think those that were not selected viewed his perception of them?
>
> _____
>
> _____
>
> _____

Not unlike this young man, some managers are oblivious to their own actions and to the fact that they are setting the standards for other people's behaviour. Remember Mary? Suppose Mary were the boss, and that she is making calls to her family in California. If a staff member observes the habit, Mary can hardly complain if that employee believes such long distance calls are acceptable behaviour. If she does, she has established that there is a double standard in the company.

Business Ethics

If Mary inflates invoices, why can't her staff?
If Mary accepts an expensive gift from a supplier, why can't they?
If Mary delays payments, why can't they?
If Mary breaches confidentiality, why can't they?

In coming to terms with the notion that you are a role model for values, you should recognise that no matter how talented, personable and efficient other employees may be — the receptionist at the front desk, the sales rep with a client, an auditor with the records — *you* set the standards for your staff's behaviour by what you say and do, not the receptionist, the sales rep or the auditor.

Step 3. Assume the responsibility for instilling ethical behaviour

The responsibility for setting ethical standards starts at the top. Certainly, you can speak about the importance of being responsible or fair, but if you yourself behave in a manner that is neither responsible nor fair, that behaviour will outweigh your words. Negative values are being transmitted to the people with whom you come in contact. Therefore, in the third step of the process assume the responsibility for being proactive about raising ethics as an issue and for knowing what you stand for.

Once you realise that you are a role model and that you have an impact on others, embarrassing or awkward though that mantle of power may feel on your shoulders, you should reflect yet again. Ask yourself what it is you stand for.

Step 4. Determine what you consider to be ethical practice

Having accepted the responsibility and the power that you have, you should analyse what you believe is acceptable practice and what is unacceptable practice in business. You need to think about what is most important to you; for example, is it profit at any cost?

How Can You Create an Ethical Working Environment?

- You need to ask yourself if you think that it is acceptable to malign the competition.
- You need to ask yourself if you would sign a contract with a company or do business in a country that has questionable work practices or human rights violations.
- You need to ask yourself what your views are on short-term expediency as opposed to long-term strategy.

To make ethics a priority and to instil values in your staff, you, as a manager, have to find the time to determine what is important to you about the way you do business. To do that, you need to think about all aspects of your business: hiring practices, advertising, accounting systems, evaluation, research, product design. Don't just think about your own area of responsibility.

Suppose, in your reflection on how you do business, you decide that you value 'treating people with dignity'. Be sure to think through what you mean by the term. What *do* you mean by 'dignity'? Which people? All those on the board? Your suppliers? Who?

Identify one value that is important to you as a manager:

_____

_____

Using the value that you selected, ask yourself whether or not the people who report to you know that the value you selected is what you stand for. For example, if you value 'treating people with dignity', does your staff know that you do?

No ☐   Yes ☐   Maybe ☐

If you responded No or Maybe, you might ask yourself why your staff don't know and then ask yourself what you might do to ensure that they will know.

Step 5. Articulate your values

Let's suppose you have accepted the notion that you are a role model. You also know what you believe is acceptable practice in business. Do you think that it is sufficient for people to draw all their conclusions about your standards from intuiting what you want them to understand? If you don't believe that intuition is sufficient, then you need to consider what mechanisms are available to you in your department and in your organisation that would allow you to share your views with your staff. How can you articulate precisely what you stand for and what you expect of them *vis-à-vis* those standards? Your staff should know precisely what your expectations are. They should not have to guess what they are, rely on innuendo or interpret your body language.

Earlier you were asked to identify one of your own values. Undoubtedly, there are others that you hold as important. In many companies, mission statements, vision statements, codes of conduct, credos or codes of practice are used as mechanisms for articulating standards and values. Typically, these documents are the codification of the values of one or of all senior management.

Let's be clear. Some of these codes are not reflections of management's thinking at all; they are boiler-plates of other companies' existing codes. If you accept the notion that we are all unique individuals and that companies are unique in their own ways, you can see how difficult it is to truly reflect your own company's values or culture by borrowing issues and language from another organisation.

What is your view of an organisation deciding to identify its mission by having a contest? Whoever wrote the best mission statement won a prize.

_____

_____

_____

How Can You Create an Ethical Working Environment?

What benefit or disadvantage might you see in such an approach to preparing a mission statement?

_____

_____

_____

While you might have said that the process is beneficial because it involves the staff, you may have also asked, 'Whose mission is it?' or 'How seriously will the mission be taken?' Frankly, it might be even more interesting to run a contest to determine whether everyone in the organisation sees the mission in the same way. Such an eventuality would give you some valuable information!*

Now let's return to the single value that you identified as being important to you. Ask yourself some additional questions: How am I going to communicate that value to my staff? Should we have a code or credo? Should it be printed on a card, etched over the door, or written in a handbook or on the back of a folder? Should I call a meeting and announce my values? Declare my convictions?

To help you answer the questions, think about how people learn. How are new ideas mastered or internalised?

One way that we learn is by rote memory. You learned many subjects that way, so using the particular value that you identified as important, you might decide that the best method for your staff to understand that value is for you to write it on a sheet of paper and to ask your staff to memorise it: 'I will be responsible to my customers,' 'Fairness is important in all dealings.'

You may see an inherent difficulty in that approach. While some organisations insist on its members being able to recite an oath, you as a manager need to be sure that well-intentioned

---

* See *101 Great Mission Statements* by Timothy R V Foster (Kogan Page, 1993)

and important statements about the way business should be done, about values, are in fact guiding meaningful behaviour. Are they saying words, or are they doing it and living by it?

How can you be sure that your values are internalised, so that your staff live and breathe not only the words, but the intent of the words, so that those words guide their actions? That difficult process of transforming words or phrases about standards or aspirations is the next step in the manager's job.

You want to instil an ethical environment. If you accept, first of all, that you are a role model and that instilling values is a part of that role, then you need to know what those values are and then articulate them. The next step involves deciding how you will transmit them to your staff so that you will all be on the same wavelength.

Step 6. Train your staff

The next step in the process of creating an ethical working environment requires some kind of training. In Chapter 1 we talked about handbooks. Some companies choose to tackle the issue of values by printing and distributing values statements. Earlier we asked you to consider how we learn and suggested that rote memory is not always the most effective means. That is particularly true about ethics which, as you know, is elusive and intangible. Therefore, it is important to create opportunities to talk about issues or to clarify them.

To ensure that your staff knows what you mean when you refer to 'dignity' or 'fairness', you need to bring your staff together to talk, and not only about targets, quotas or new photocopiers. You should also have meetings about how you do business, about the ethics of how you are doing business.

Perhaps because you think that your staff will not recognise ethical dilemmas or won't know how to handle them, you may want to set aside time to discuss a real work situation or case study that includes an ethical problem. Perhaps you are aware of a situation that has just happened in the office, and you want to get your staff's views on how it should have been or was handled.

How Can You Create an Ethical Working Environment?

If you find a significant disparity in viewpoints as to what was the right way to handle the problem, then as a manager, you will have learned that each individual is making decisions based on his or her own value system, not necessarily on the one that you believe should be the standard for your organisation. If that's the case, you might want to consider whether the notion of 'values in general' should be an agenda item, one that is just as important as whether or not to purchase a new telephone system. You might want to consider holding a workshop on solving ethical dilemmas or holding a meeting to discuss a particular ethical situation and how it might be resolved. Would a discussion about the values of the organisation be useful in your company?

Once you have decided that ethics belongs on the table, not in the back corner of the closet, and that there is some consensus about what you mean by 'dignity' or by 'fairness', then you should examine what mechanisms there are for members of the department or division to communicate their concerns about a particular problem. If you, as a manager, want to foster ethical thinking, you have to model your concern for it, you have to show your staff that it is important to you.

Step 7. Encourage open communication

You have to foster communication among your staff. They need to feel free to bring issues involving standards, values, and ethics to you without fear of reprisal. They should be able to blow the whistle internally on a faulty design or product or on an inappropriate practice without fear of losing their jobs or damaging their careers.

To create an ethical environment, you should be sensitive to the realities of communication. You must get to know how information is transmitted within your organisation. Are people coming to you with their problems or concerns or are they whinging, like John, and taking those concerns home? Might the problem between Sally and John have been averted? How are you perceived as a boss? Are you approachable, or are you threatening? Are issues of values important to you? Are they *seen* to be of importance to you? Do you make the time to deal with them? Do you need relief from your responsibilities or do you need support from another source to meet that need?

Some larger organisations are creating positions, the sole function of which is to address problems relating to ethics. Although such organisations are acknowledging the need for someone to have the time to address ethics, you can also see a downside: that the manager is somewhat removed from the process. You may have created such a position or supported it, but your removal from it sends a message that ethics is a tangential issue. It's important, yes, but the message conveyed is that you have more important issues to deal with.

Step 8. Be consistent

The final step in creating an ethical working environment is to ensure that people are being consistent and open. How can you do that? You have recognised your responsibility. You have articulated your views of what is right. You have worked on creating an environment in which people are willing to share their concerns about value issues. You have to be sure that there are systems in place that will allow you to punish or reprimand if those values are not maintained. You cannot say, 'Henceforth there will be no conflict of interest' and then have no system in place to govern how you are going to handle a situation in which a conflict of interest occurs. You need to ensure that, if your company's standards are violated, the individual who has breached the code will pay an appropriate price for that inappropriate behaviour. If there are no consequences to unethical actions, you are modelling the fact that what you say has nothing to do with what you do.

How Can You Create an Ethical Working Environment?

Insurance that standards are being met should be just as visible in whatever performance appraisal system you have in place. If you evaluate people on their decision-making or on their productivity, are you also evaluating them on their confidentiality or just on their attendance?

You can see that we all have standards and that they are diverse. You can also see that each of us comes to the workplace with a variety of needs and motivations that may cause us to act unethically even though we have been taught to behave otherwise.

As this century nears its end, we are becoming more aware of how actions in one part of the world may impact on another. If you wish to stay competitive in this difficult market, ethics and excellence are essential to your ongoing success. Managers themselves have a significant role to play in that process. Consider the following eight steps:

1. Make the decision to commit to ethics
2. Recognise that you are a role model by definition, by your actions and by your values
3. Assume the responsibility for instilling ethical behaviour
4. Determine what you consider to be ethical practice
5. Articulate your values
6. Train your staff
7. Encourage open communication
8. Be consistent.

In essence, to create an ethical environment you have to reflect on your role as a manager and on the relationships that you have and want to keep with all your stakeholders. You should assume the responsibility for instilling ethical behaviour, determine what you consider to be ethical practice, then articulate those values. Having done that, it is time to ensure that your staff are trained to recognise, understand and handle ethical dilemmas and to see that they genuinely work by the values that you have articulated. To be sure that your message is understood, you should encourage open communication and be consistent in your dealings.

Business Ethics

As a manager you have a significant role to play in creating an ethical environment. Your commitment to values should serve you well as a business person. It should also serve you well as a person.

Further Reading from Kogan Page

Better Management Skills

This highly popular range of inexpensive paperbacks covers all areas of basic management. Practical, easy to read and instantly accessible, these guides will help managers to improve their business or communication skills. Those marked * are available on audio cassette.

The books in this series can be tailored to specific company requirements. For further details, please contact the publisher, Kogan Page, telephone 0171 278 0433, fax 0171 837 6348.

Be a Successful Supervisor
Business Etiquette
Business Creativity
Coaching Your Employees
Conducting Effective Interviews
Counselling Your Staff
Creative Decision-Making
Creative Thinking in Business
Effective Employee Participation
Effective Meeting Skills
Effective Performance Appraisals*
Effective Presentation Skills
Empowerment

Business Ethics

First Time Supervisor
Get Organised!
Goals and Goal Setting
How to Communicate Effectively*
How to Develop a Positive Attitude*
How to Develop Assertiveness
How to Motivate People*
How to Understand Financial Statements
How to Write a Staff Manual
Improving Employee Performance
Improving Relations at Work
Keeping Customers for Life
Leadership Skills for Women
Learning to Lead
Make Every Minute Count*
Making TQM Work
Managing Cultural Diversity at Work
Managing Disagreement Constructively
Managing Organisational Change
Managing Part-time Employees
Managing Quality Customer Service
Managing Your Boss
Marketing for Success
Memory Skills in Business
Mentoring
Office Management
Personnel Testing
Productive Planning
Project Management
Quality Customer Service
Rate Your Skills as a Manager
Sales Training Basics
Self-Managing Teams
Selling Professionally
Successful Negotiation
Successful Presentation Skills
Successful Telephone Techniques
Systematic Problem-Solving and Decision-Making

Further Reading from Kogan Page

Team Building
Training Methods that Work
The Woman Manager